I0004532

A Post-Mortem

Review

by

Karl A. Cox, PhD.

Preface

This book applies the techniques found in the book Strategic Requirements Analysis: from interviews to models [1] by myself to a post-mortem review of a failed project. It's a real case that transpired 10 years ago and I have changed the details to hide the actual company, people and location.

You may note that there are a few references to part of the Strategic Requirements book in terms of understanding and explaining techniques such as how to build a goal model and how to prepare and run an interview, or how to do analysis of the interview and how to create a context model. All the "how to" is found in the Strategic Requirements Analysis book. Here I document a case study of a real post-mortem review that I took part in conducting. I do elaborate upon the "how to" when it gets to the specifics of post-mortem reviews in how they differ from strategic IT project analysis for new projects (not failed projects!).

Introduction

The following case study is that of a root cause analysis of a system failure. A post-mortem[1] is a different context to that of a standard IT project. If you get hired or are asked to conduct a post-mortem review, normally it is because something went wrong with the release or delivery or there was a major issue during the project that caused or nearly caused a derailment and runaway. There are other examples of when you might be asked to conduct a review, for instance, in validating a specification document: an IT manager may be unconvinced by a requirements specification – there might be too many requirements pushing the estimated cost of delivery beyond the allocated budget – and may call you to conduct an analysis of it. You will want to interview the key stakeholders so will plan as normal. The focus of the interview will be to extract out the real requirements and then compare your findings to those of the original specification. The focus for us, though, is of a post-mortem review. In other words, an engagement to find out what went wrong after a software product was released onto the market or internally to the company or to existing customers, causing for example significant financial and data loss.

[1] Other terms are interchangeable: post-implementation, post-incident. I will stick with post-mortem because it is the most common term.

Case Study Background

The case examines a strategic IT failure where a government agency outsources its customer-facing IT to Brightmouth Solutions[2]. This case explores the business as well as technical reasons for failure and proposes solutions that should halt the systemic problems in both the Agency and Brightmouth.

Brightmouth Solutions Post-Mortem Review Context

Brightmouth Solutions is a software provider that delivers cloud and web systems to a large government agency that manages vehicle license, insurance and registration renewals. Every quarter Brightmouth releases updates, patches, fixes, new features and new applications to existing software suites that are used by both the Agency employees and its customers, citizens of this country. The latest release of a product with the Agency, at the most critical point in the financial year, caused severe problems across one hundred customer-facing offices, bringing them to a standstill. As a result, customers were unable to complete their business before the end of the tax year causing some of them to run into potential financial penalties, be arrested and lose jobs. The result, in this case, was headline news – not good for the software provider, not good for the Agency and terrible for its customers. Brightmouth Solutions has a recent history of making public mistakes and its paymasters, the Agency, are considering withdrawing from the very long-term contract it has with the provider unless immediate steps are taken to remedy the situation. Karl Land Ltd has been hired by both Brightmouth Solutions and the Agency to find out what went wrong and how to fix it.

The following Table 1 presents a completed global checklist by Karl Land Ltd's lead consultant in preparation for the engagement with Brightmouth Solutions.

---

[2] Thanks to Bob Hughes and Mike Cotterell for the name of Brightmouth which I borrow from their excellent book, Software Project Management, McGraw-Hill, 5th Edition 2009.

Table 1. Global checklist for Brightmouth Solutions

#	Item	Answer	Responsible & contact	Issues
1	What is the overriding objective for the engagement?	Identify the root causes of the failure, their impact and propose viable contextual long-term solutions to eradicate the root causes both at Brightmouth and the Agency.	karlC@KL, MC@Brightmouth, (CEO) RH@Agency (Director)	Contracted to both parties may well lead to conflict of interest and risk over payment but have been assured this will not be the case.
2	What is the context of the engagement?	See attachment. In brief: Documented failure to re-issue licenses and registration docs at Agency (see press clipping) has led to major strategic review of business processes and IT supply between and by Brightmouth Solutions.	karlC@KL MC@Brightmouth, (CEO) RH@Agency (Director)	Review and recommendations must be implemented prior to next release (9 weeks away). My view is this is unlikely.
3	Who are you going to interview?	See list attached – range looks to be from executives to operations in both organisations.	MC@Brightmouth, (CEO) RH@Agency (Director) administrators	Large numbers listed (25) and this may grow to 30+. Looks comprehensive in coverage. Will

				have to reconsider timeframe, scope and finances.
4	Who are the high priority interviewees?	Am keen to talk with customer service reps and customer rep as they are front line. So what they say may hold sway over internal viewpoints.	-	None
5	In what order should you interview people?	See attached list.	MC@Brightmouth, (CEO) RH@Agency (Director) administrators	Would like to talk to customer service reps and customers at Agency before talking with Brightmouth. Need to know impact and effect on confidence.
6	When should the interview happen?	See attached schedule.	MC@Brightmouth, (CEO) RH@Agency (Director) administrators	Looks ok though 5-6 interviews per day may be too much for 1st week.
7	Where should the interview take place?	Have set up an interview room at Agency and at Brightmouth.	MC@Brightmouth, (CEO) RH@Agency (Director) administrators	Will have to check in advance about location of rooms and set up (facilities).
8	What equipment	Usual [pens,	karlC@KL	Make sure iPod

	should you take into an interview?	notebook, iPod].		charged with cable.
9	Who arranges the interviews?	Done. Both admin have done this.	MC@Brightmouth, (CEO) RH@Agency (Director) administrators	Check with interviewees in advance they know their schedule.
10	What is an optimal number of interviews for your engagement?	Decided: 25 selected in advance; anticipate 5 or so more.	karlC@KL	Will need approval from both Agency and Brightmouth if extra interviews start to take up too much time?
11	How long do you have to do the interviews?	2 weeks scheduled but this is for interviews themselves. Will need 2 extra weeks to conduct analysis.	karlC@KL, MC & RH	Will need to ask for leeway if analysis gets particularly complex (e.g. 1-2 extra weeks).
12	Will there by follow ups / feedback?	Yes to follow ups but only minimal. No to feedback – need to await official report.	karlC@KL, MC & RH	None
13	How many interviewers do you need?	2 in total – check Jane is available.	karlC@KL	If Jane unavailable for all, then check if Marian can sit in when Jane can't be there.
14	Are there special instructions from	None thus far – no impression there	karlC@KL, MC & RH	None.

your client about the interview plan or subsequent phases?	will be.		

Table 2 presents an Interview Specific list for an interview at Brightmouth Solutions.

Table 2. Interview Specific List example Brightmouth Solutions

Interviewee: Mike, GM of IT, sits on User Relations Board as technical advisor Location: BS L4.17 Time: 16:00 Date: Mon 10 Jan 2015		Interviewers: Karl and Jane
#	**Item**	**Answers**
1	What are the key objectives for this interview?	1. Understand business of Brightmouth and its relationship with the Agency. 2. Establish what went wrong on this release from Brightmouth perspective. 3. Identify any impacts, symptoms, observations and opportunities.
2	What is the specific context for this interview?	First interview at Brightmouth. Need to know about the bigger picture and background. Learn about Brightmouth Solutions and its relationship with the Agency. Try to understand how Brightmouth does its IT and supports its clients. Try to get information on Brightmouth's processes, practices, what went wrong, why and what the history of problems at Brightmouth really is.
3	What questions are you going to ask?	1. Tell me about Brightmouth Solutions. (Help understand interview objective 1.) 2. Tell me the history of the relationship with the

		Agency (Interview objective 1.)
		3. Describe your role in relationship with Agency. (Objectives 1 and 2.)
		4. Walk me through a standard release process from your perspective. (Objectives 1, 2 and 3.)
		5. What practices do you have in place at Brightmouth e.g. such as following / adhering to standards like ISO or ITIL? (Objectives 2 and 3.)
		6. Tell me about this particular release, what went wrong and how would you fix it? (Objective 3.)
4	Follow up with interviewee?	Definitely assuming a willingness to do so – key role at Brightmouth.
5	What promises can you make to an interviewee?	TBD – depends on CEOs.
6	Modifying the plan as you learn more.	1st interview at Brightmouth – may suggest change in order of interviews or who to talk to who isn't on the list?

Root Cause Analysis

Root Cause Analysis is an approach to identifying key causes of failure that may be systemic to a process that is institutionalised or may be a one-off event. Normally, if you identify and eradicate the systemic problem, you are more likely to eliminate opportunities for one-off gaffs. A root cause analysis consists of the following steps as presented in the flow chart in figure 1.

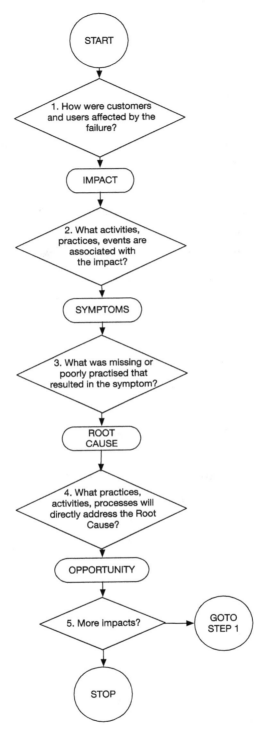

Figure 1. Root Cause Analysis flowchart

The steps in figure 1 are elaborated upon in table 3.

Table 3. Root Cause Analysis

Step	To identify	Explanation	Possible questions to ask
1	Impact	Impact affects customers and end users. An impact is anything that affects a capability, results in an end-customer/user outcome, or either inhibits or promotes the achievement of a business goal or strategy.	Where, when, how were customers and end users affected by the system failure? Who specifically? For how long? Was the business affected? How? How was this resolved? What are the long term implications?
2	Symptom	Symptoms are what stakeholders identify as contributing to the impact. Symptoms express states, conditions, incidents, and activities. Incidents may be one-offs or repeated.	Why did the impact happen? Was this a regular practice or rogue? Were there any unusual/different circumstances prior to the failure?
3	Root Cause	A Root Cause is a missing or faulty key practice that is within the realm of control of the organization to which symptoms can be logically traced and impacts can be rationally explained. Extrapolate Root Cause by identifying a missing key practice that results in the	What specifically about the regular practice is a concern? Is there something missing that should be there? How do you know this specific activity is responsible? Can we replicate the activity? Does this precisely explain the cause of the impact or was there something additional or

		symptoms and are tied to the impacts.	did we miss something?
4	Opportunity	Opportunities are long term solutions: best practices and processes and entirely context specific. Propose Opportunities to address the Root Cause, thereby alleviating the Symptoms and neutralizing negative Impacts.	Given 'x' Root Cause, what can we do to stop / fix / remove / improve this state? Is there anything we missed?

Table 3 above indicates a root cause analysis conducted after a major incident will quickly yield results that can be acted upon. Actually this is rarely the case. Often stakeholders struggle to get past their prejudices to get to the heart of the real problems. This is understandable and something you will need to take into consideration. The problem is that typically you will be an outsider to the project even if part of the same company and will not know enough, yet, to identify the facts from the obsessions.

You also have to avoid presenting back 'motherhood' statements such as, 'poor project management' or 'lack of requirements process'. It is likely that your client knows this already. You need to be more specific about your observations in order to convince your client: what specific project management / requirements management practice and/or process activities were missing or poor? Why did it matter?

Prior to the following interview, I'll start by presenting some background context that you should have already established prior to the interview from your reading, and identified objectives for the interview itself.

Interview: Brightmouth Solutions Ltd

Context

Brightmouth Solutions is a software provider that delivers cloud and web systems to government agencies and updates systems, when needed as part of a quarterly release cycle. The latest release at the most critical point in the financial year caused severe problems over 100 customer-facing offices, bringing them to a standstill. Customers were then unable to complete their business before the end of the tax year causing some of them to run into potential financial penalties, a number of arrests and loss of jobs. The result, in this case, was headline news – not good for the software provider, not good for the government and terrible for its customers. Brightmouth Solutions has a recent history of making public mistakes and its paymasters, the government, are considering withdrawing from the contract it has with the provider unless immediate steps are taken to remedy the situation. Karl Land Ltd has been hired by Brightmouth Solutions in conjunction with the Agency to find out what went wrong and how to fix it.

Engagement Objective

Identify the root causes of the failure, their impact and propose viable contextual long-term solutions to eradicate the root causes both at Brightmouth and the Agency.

Interviewee

Mike, is the General Manager of IT at Brightmouth Solutions. He is a skilled enterprise architect, working on a daily basis with the IT team. He also sits on the User Relations Board as a technical advisor; hence he has direct contact with his users. As a GM, Mike also reports regularly to the executive.

Throughout the interview transcript, comments are added in [...comment...] to show how Mike's answers will help in the overall engagement objective. These will refer back to the flowchart in figure 1 to show when information has been extracted relevant to the flowchart and the context information in Table 2.

The Interview Transcript

Me: Tell me about your business, Mike.

[Comment: once into the main event there is no messing about. This obviously addresses the third interview objective.]

Mike: Brightmouth Solutions provide cloud and web systems for numerous government agencies that act as a single entry point to various government agency services such as renewing passports, driving licenses, making appointments at various medical centres – that's new – and providing a wealth of information. We also provide a number of agencies with intranets, software applications, infrastructure and even hardware.

[Comment: Remember the point of asking this question is to confirm your understanding of the context of the business. Why does this matter? It is fundamental to your job to know what is going on in a broader sense than just the engagement. You need to be able to communicate with interviewees and clients as if you had been working in their company for the last five years. This puts your interviewees at ease, they will confide in you more if they feel comfortable talking with you; your findings will make much more sense and your recommendations will fit with the needs and culture of the client business.]

Me: What is your role?

Mike: My title is General Manager of Technology. I oversee all technical roll outs, including this current release – what a release that was too.

Me: Really? Can we come back to that in a minute? I also understand you liaise with your customers in an official capacity?

[Comment: I cut Mike off from pursuing what might be a significant subject matter – for now. It's important to be able to do this because you need to get the context in place first before you go after the details. You run the risk of slightly bemusing your interviewees but it is worth it. Just don't forget to go back to that significant point – if you ultimately believe it is significant – later in the interview. In this case, it is. It is important to ensure your understanding of the context is right first; this will allow you to contextualise your questions and your findings.]

Mike: That's right. I sit on the monthly User Relations Board as technical advisor. I report back to my CIO who reports to the CEO. This means that what I report back from customer representatives and their management tends to get to the very top. This last meeting was not a lot of fun – I really got it in the neck – but at least the CEO and CIO have seen there's something wrong with what we are doing and are going to change things around a bit.
[Comment: now you understand the chain of command and the relationship between provider and customer.]

Me: What happened after the release?
[Comment: back to the 'nugget' and begins to address interview objective 1.]

Mike: Nothing.

Me: Nothing?

Mike: At least for three weeks during which time we had sufficient volume of traffic to assume nothing was going to go wrong.

Me: So what went wrong?

Mike: Technically: our servers froze, printers stalled and we couldn't process transactions fast enough. Let me give you a scenario: a customer wants to renew their driving license. A clerk in one of our one hundred or more outlets would type the license number into the system---
[Comment: we are addressing interview objective 1 about impacts. Technical impacts: servers frozen, printers stalling; human impact: staff unable to complete customer transaction.]

Me: The customer is there or doing this over the phone?

Mike: Both and via an online service that isn't as automated as we would quite like. Anyway, the clerk would type in the license number, the renew process worked as expected but there was a delay in printing the actual new license. A delay is normal of say three to five minutes when we are busy but we started to get a build up of delays of thirty to forty minutes.

[Comment: there is some more context here on how transactions can be conducted. Here is a detail of the impact on the customer: a delay of thirty to forty minutes in printing the licenses.]

Me: That's not good news.

Mike: No it wasn't.

Me: So how did the customer react?

Mike: Not very well, you can imagine. Most people renew their license the day the old one is due to expire. The process shouldn't take more than fifteen minutes.

Me: So you're saying some licenses didn't get renewed in time?

Mike: That's exactly what I'm saying. We had customers queuing out the door. And then we had to close the door on a lot of them. They didn't get licenses renewed and suddenly the next morning we had a handful of customers getting fines for driving without a valid license. Other drivers, many of them delivery men, simply didn't risk it and ended up delivering late. Some drove illegally and gambled they wouldn't get pulled over, being told by their bosses to deliver or don't come back to work again. And some of those were stopped by police and guess what, no valid license. So they are going to lose their jobs anyway. The police called us and said they had a lot of unlicensed drivers complaining about the failure we had. Fortunately, we could verify this because some of our staff were smart enough to take names and license numbers of queuing customers in case something like this happened. I suppose the customer told them he was going to drive irrespective but wanted a get out of jail card if pulled over or in an accident.

[Comment: here is the nub of the impact: Customers driving without licenses and customers not driving at all, many at risk of losing their job, getting into trouble with the police or both. Note that no root causes have been identified yet. This is not unusual in these circumstances. It often takes further investigations to identify a technical or practice root cause whose impact is felt in the world.]

Me: When the delays began in the outlets, what did the staff do to notify anyone?
[Comment: I've shifted focus from customer to staff in the agency outlets in order to identify further impacts, symptoms and hopefully root causes.]

Mike: They would have informed their office manager and that person would have called a help desk.

Me: OK. 'A' help desk? Not 'the'?

Mike: They have more than one. It depends on the nature of the problem which one to call or which number you happen to dial.

Me: Each desk has a different number?

Mike: Yes.
[Comment: a symptom. The different help desks, each with its own contact number, are a potential symptom of the impact; we are not sure yet what the impact is, so we need to find out more.]

Me: When were you notified of the problem? And who told you?

Mike: I got a direct call from one of the Customer Board members on Saturday morning – the release went live Thursday night – saying there was a big problem. I checked my technical team immediately. They said all was well as far they were told.

[Comment: this reaffirms our suspicion that the various help desks are part of the problem or symptomatic of a systemic failure. Given the role of the help desk is to record incidents, among other things, and send these on to the IT provider, it appears they did not do this efficiently enough; this is the impact: unnecessary delay in notification of the problem. This might sound like a root cause: time taken to notify technical team is too long but we need to ask why it took so long because, remember, Mike was first informed of the problem not by the Help Desk but by a personal contact. Verification with his IT team contradicted this information. Something is wrong with the Help Desks. So I ask some more questions.]

Me: Do you do performance monitoring of your system?

Mike: No. We rely on our customers to tell us.

Me: So when did they tell you?

Mike: Other than that phone call, we got our first notice – in the incident log – about two days after the event.

Me: Two days? That seems a bit too late.
[Comment: here is a symptom – notification of an issue took two days to filter through to the technical team. Why is this? There's more to ask about first.]

Mike: Yes, it is.

Me: I've been told that the issue was resolved in fifteen days. Was it that complex a problem?

Mike: No, not at all. It took about three days to unravel the problem and a day to fix.

Me: But it took fifteen days to resolve? What happened to those eleven days?
[Comment: here seems to be another systemic problem emerging... more impacts but what are the symptoms and causes?]

Mike: Ah, well, we got the notification from our customer and then decided it wasn't high priority so sat on it.

Me: What made you decide it was not a high priority?

Mike: All we got was one incident report of a slow license printer.
[Comment: here is the symptom of the impact: one incident report was sent; hence the non-reaction from the technical team.]

Me: But wasn't this affecting all the outlets?

Mike: Correct. The trouble with the report is that the Help Desk staff collate all the calls and put it into one report.

Me: So they might get ten individual reports but only send you one notice?

Mike: Correct again. In this case, something like three thousand printers went wrong. [Comment: symptom again.]

Me: What about the two help desks?

Mike: This was a problem – by the way there are three but customers can only find two phone numbers on the website. Office staff can call the third number if they find it on the intranet.

Me: Three? And three separate numbers?

Mike: They had customers calling two of the numbers and employees calling all three. The Help Desk people collated the calls first and put them into the incident log, well one of them did. The second used some CRM software they had installed that sends out text files to everyone. The third just sent us emails.

[Comment: more symptoms. It has become clear that a symptom of the impact (fix took fifteen day to roll out because of eleven-day delay in responding) is the way that notification of incidents are dealt with and sent to Mike's team. What is the root cause? Let's find out more.]

Me: Did the calls stop?

Mike: No, but the weekend intervened so there was just a hiatus. I only fathomed there was a real problem when I got that phone call plus my sister told me about her license woes over Sunday dinner. I thought she was exaggerating when she said she'd been queuing for four hours and had then given up. But I checked it out with a couple of the outlet managers and found a big fat mess.
[Comment: queuing for four hours is a customer impact. There appears to be a major communications problem. Failure to communicate effectively in relaying messages from the three help desks to the technical team is a major impact. The root cause of the impact is there are too many help desks each with its own way of processing incidents.]

Me: So how would you fix this problem in communication: the three help desks, the way in which incidents are reported?
[Comment: we are now trying to pinpoint Opportunities to address this root cause – interview objective 2.]

Mike: First of all, why have three help desks? I don't understand that at all. OK, so it is an historical thing but I believe the Agency should change this. One help desk is enough. This would resolve the way each desk communicated. In we can't have the single help desk we need a single system that all share to report incidents in real time: an incident comes into the help desk, it gets logged and if it isn't resolved there and then, we get told about it immediately. The real problem was the collation of the same incidents – over a hundred incidents of printer failure, server failure, all with the same characteristics.
[Comment: Opportunity – centralise the help desks into one; put in one system for reporting incidents.]

Me: But you might get one hundred calls on one very minor issue and only ten on something more important; which one gets priority?

Mike: You are quite right. We need a way to address this.

Me: So what really happened?

Mike: Well, this seems to have been our fault to some extent. We regularly rewrite pieces of code to make our applications more scalable, robust, or add features etcetera. In this particular case, one of the systems engineers modified a printer driver module to make it compatible to some other environment. Unwittingly, he unblocked an email-sending module at the same time. The code got to be released without being effectively tested by Quality Assurance. This happens from time to time. For a reason we are yet to fathom and may never do, the newly released printer driver enabled the email capability so that at every single request to print a new license the printer driver first polled every single email address on our servers to compare the one associated with the license to be printed with every email in our databases to check if it was an invalid email address. This meant that the waiting time at the printers got greater and greater the more printer requests were being sent through from different printers each one demanded that each email on our files be checked with the applicant's one to see if it was invalid. The servers were degrading in performance as more and more email checks were being sent. Eventually we came to a standstill.
[Comment: the technical impact: a print function that checked for invalid email addresses, causing the server performance to degrade and printing to stop.]

Me: So not only was there a freak and catastrophic technical problem, but there are also issues with quality assurance and configuration management?
[Comment: This appears to be the symptom: untested code released into a live product. It's probably a symptom of something going wrong with the Quality Assurance procedures or practices. This is something to note and return to later. For now we want to pursue the technical issue.]

Mike: Correct.

Me: If you don't mind, I'd like to dig a little deeper about the technical issue and return to the quality assurance and, presumably, configuration management issue a little later.

Mike: Sure.

...

And on it goes. Mike mentioned there were issues with quality assurance and configuration management. Now is the opportunity to revisit that part of the conversation:

Me: I just wanted to go over a point you made to be sure I understood it correctly... let me see what I've written down.
[Comment: don't read it aloud, you are buying yourself a few seconds extra thinking time.]

Me: Could I clarify one point you made, the cause of failure you think was because code got released into the system that hadn't been tested.
[Comment: this is reconfirming the important point made earlier by Mike.]

Mike: That's what I believe happened.

Me: How did that code slip into the release without being tested?

Mike: Actually it was tested by the developer so as a unit it functioned but when it was integrated into the live system, that's when we got problems. It wasn't really the integration so much as the impact of its introduction.

Me: Not regression tested?
[Comment: We are getting to a root cause though here we have a symptom. New code is integrated and released without regression testing[3].]

Mike: That's right, we didn't test the impact of the new code before releasing it. As I said earlier, normally code is put into the configuration management [CM] system and QA gets it farmed out to them from there. But I think it is slow: the CM system is unreliable and the process seems to change on a weekly basis so sometimes code gets passed direct to QA, bypassing CM. It's possible that code could have been sent back to CM for release without QA checking it if it didn't originate from CM. There are so many ways to bypass CM that I'm amazed it hasn't happened more regularly.

[Comment: there appears to be more than one root cause. Lack of a clear and defined rigorously applied regression testing strategy is one. The other is ill-defined configuration management. We might be tempted to combine these weaknesses and call it the end-to-end testing process so long as we are not losing specificity.]

Me: So the problem you see is the process of signing in code into the CM system is cumbersome so people tend to ignore that step and go direct to QA. Code then gets mixed up – was it tested, wasn't it? There wasn't a config label on it to say—
[Comment: I am trying to establish the process for code to go from the coder into the product. This gives me context to the problem. I am establishing more symptoms.]

Mike: There isn't an automated CM label but there is a note from the CM manager saying the status of the code in the release cycle... usually.
[Comment: a symptom – 'usually', meaning sometimes this does not happen.]

Me: Sometimes there isn't?

Mike: That's right. It's still a manual process and sometimes code gets sent out with no info attached.

---

[3] Regression testing: testing for errors in software when new code is introduced into an existing software program by testing a core of features to see if they still function in the same way. With a change in a printer driver, it would make sense to regression test the printer functions. Whether a large scale test of printers can be conducted is another issue.

[Comment: here's a symptom that there is a dysfunctional configuration management process.]

Me: Really?

Mike: Really.

Me: -- and this being a bigger than normal release, people were pressed and so the code got sent back into CM untested from QA and then released?

Mike: That's right.
[Comment: and another problem – the release turns out to be larger than normal...]

Post-mortem Review Analysis

The first step in the post-mortem review analysis is to conduct a content analysis of the interviews. This is important in identifying the flow of impacts, current practices (symptoms), systemic practice problems (root causes) and opportunities for long term solutions. The content analysis is shown in table 4. The background for post-mortem review interviews and how to recognise impacts, symptoms, root causes and opportunities is discussed above. The context of the engagement is repeated here:

"Brightmouth Solutions is a software provider that delivers cloud and web systems to government agencies and updates systems, when needed as part of a quarterly release cycle. The latest release at the most critical point in the financial year caused severe problems over one hundred customer-facing offices, bringing them to a standstill. Customers were then unable to complete their business before the end of the tax year causing some of them to run into potential financial penalties, arrests and loss of jobs at a time when the economy was slumping. The result, in this case, was headline news – not good for the software provider, not good for the government and terrible for its customers. Brightmouth Solutions has a recent history of making public mistakes and its paymasters, the government, are considering withdrawing from the contract it has with the provider unless immediate steps are taken to remedy the situation."

As can be seen, Table 4 is populated with responses from the example interview with Mike, General Manager of IT at Brightmouth Solutions, as well as interviews from stakeholders within the Agency and a customer representative, who all provide their own perspectives on the failure.

Table 5 is a root cause analysis table. It is populated with direct responses from the content analysis in a similar fashion to that of a strategic analysis. Table 6 is structured in themed rows to reflect the main areas to have emerged from the interviews of identified impact: technical, customers and Help Desks. It's a good idea to structure the analysis like this because this sharpens our focus. Don't forget, though, that there are dependencies between these themes as well as overlaps. The point of separation is to make our lives a little easier and ultimately to be able to provide more cleanly scoped feedback to your client.

Table 4. Content Analysis on Brightmouth Solutions interviews

Question / Role	Q1. What happened / went wrong? Impact.	Q2: Why did it happen / go wrong? Symptoms.
Mike, GM of IT at Brightmouth Solutions	(1) Servers froze; printers stopped; staff couldn't process transactions (30-40 min delay); (2) customers couldn't renew licenses and (3) risked losing jobs and (4) police fines.	(2) Three help desks failed to inform IT of severity of impact; took 2 days to notify; IT did not recognise severity because of structure of report so ignored it; (1) code released untested; process issues
Government Agency Senior Executive	(1) All 120 outlets brought to a standstill at busiest period of year; (4) Customers arrested; (5) police chief complained to government minister; (6) minister gave us ultimatum to fix it or else.	IT from Brightmouth always rubbish: since outsourcing entire IT operation to Brightmouth there have been problems because of (1) poor testing and (3) they are unaccountable if something goes wrong.

Help Desk Manager	Outlet managers called us nonstop about (1) printer freeze; (7) we escalated incident but got no response from Brightmouth so (8) could not respond to outlet staff.	(2) Communication with Brightmouth poor: 3 different routes (4) but not sure who is responsible at Brightmouth; (5) recording of incidents haphazard; (2) No standard priority and escalation process means we cannot talk about severity.
Outlet Operator	(9) Many customers couldn't renew licenses in time. (1) Our printers froze and computers died so couldn't print licenses normally: took 40 mins longer; (10) Left customers queuing out of the doors for 4-6 hours; (8) no one told us anything.	(6) Help desk redundant because they are not informed of releases until night before; we (7) have to learn the new systems and features on the job; (1) no one tested the software; (8) couldn't tell customers anything because Help Desk couldn't tell us either.
Customer Representative	(3) We lost jobs, (4) arrested, got fines. (10) Left queuing in vain for hours; (8) no advice support or help from outlet staff – they were in the dark too. (11) Help desks confusing and not responding in same way.	(4) Staff failed to pass on any new information – all their systems died. (8) No one seemed to be helping staff for 2 weeks (4) So staff and customers left in the dark.

Table 4 continued.

Question / Role	Q3: What are the systemic practices that led to it going wrong? Root causes.	Q4: How would you improve / change the current situation to avoid this happening again? Opportunities.
Mike, GM of IT at Brightmouth Solutions	(1) Help desks not collaborating and using different systems; (2) QA process broken: Configuration Management system unreliable and easily bypassed	(1) One consolidated help desk (2) single system; (3) real-time logging, notification of incidents; (4) prioritize severity and response procedure; (5) fix release management cycle, QA and CM process.
Government Agency Senior Executive	(3) Service levels and responsibilities suspicious. Service Level Agreements should be renegotiated. (2) Brightmouth test and (4) release strategies are failing customer.	(6) Rewrite service agreements to include punishment clauses for failures like this one. (5) Introduce stricter test strategy and release management practices.
Help Desk Manager	(5) No single agreed communications protocol; (1) 3 disparate competing systems; (5) no structure or clear process for reporting severity of incidents.	(1) One help desk with (2) a single incident reporting system; (4) process and/or communications protocol especially for corresponding with Brightmouth IT.
Outlet Operator	(4) Software release strategy failure; (5) communications protocol breakdown; (6) no training provision for outlet staff	(8) Timely communications process to educated staff about releases in plenty of time. (7) Staff training before release.

Customer Representative	(5) Communication procedures a problem; also there appears to be (6) no staff training.	(4) Establish emergency response procedures and communications channels in the event of failure.

Analysis of Content

Note the numbers presented in the analysis below, for example, (5) represent those items identified in table 4.

Question 1: this question asks about the impact of the failure and the responses are unequivocal and varied. The technical failure: (1) printer delay and computers not functioning causing a thirty to forty minute delay per customer. Clearly the technology failure is the immediate source of the problem. It is still an impact because these failures are the result of something else that was wrong, that is, a symptom. We enter this impact into the root cause analysis table 5.

The knock on Customer impact is that (10) customers were left queuing for hours (two responses), (2) customers could not renew licenses before the deadline (two responses) meaning some customers were arrested and received fines (three responses), and (3) some lost jobs (two responses). Although responses vary between two and three for each you cannot assume that a two is less significant than a three-response. A degree of common sense tells you that losing your job because you couldn't renew your license is in fact pretty significant, as it was for customers arrested because they had no current license. Let's enter these into table 5 as well but as one combined entry to highlight the customer impact.

Outlet Staff were obviously impacted, having to deal with irate customers. We have three interviewees commenting on staff (8) not being told what to do or how to respond, coupled with the Help Desk Manager's comment that though (7) the problem was escalated to Brightmouth they got no response and the Customer Representative commented that the (11) Help Desks were not responding in a similar manner to incidents. These impacts revolve around the Help Desk and are combined as an entry in table 5.

The Agency Senior Executive also comments that there are political ramifications: (5) the police chief complaint to the minister and the minister's angry response to the agency to sort the mess out or else. But these are not included in the table because they are a consequence of the impact.

Question 2: addresses symptoms, such as current practices (typically not to be recommended) that helped cause the impacts. The basic question is why did things go wrong? What do the Agency and/or Brightmouth Solutions regularly do that ultimately caused these impacts?

Technical: it appears that there are software testing symptoms: three interviewees state that (1) poorly or non-tested software was released. Mike also discussed (1) software process problems. There is also a concern about (3) Brightmouth's accountability if something goes wrong.

Customer: outlet staff could not get any messages to customers about the situation and how it could be resolved because (8) staff were not informed about the current situation by the Help Desk. Effectively, customers were left in the dark because (4) staff could not pass on any information. Staff that directly interact with customers are also expected (7) to self-learn new software features on the job, potentially causing delays and errors.

Help Desk: (2) three help desks all managed not to convince Brightmouth of the severity of the problem and have non-standard processes for escalation of incidents. The Help Desks themselves have problems over identifying (4) who is responsible at Brightmouth Solutions for responding to issues. The (5) recording of incidents is haphazard and the (6) help desk is considered redundant because they are not informed of releases until the night before so cannot inform the outlet staff of any changes to software or new applications – note the symptom from the Customer track that staff are expected (7) to self-learn new software features on the job. This seems almost institutionalized behaviour.

Question 3: identifies root causes. These are systemic practices and problems that are responsible for the symptoms that ultimately lead to the failure impacts.

Technical: there are number of root causes related to different impacts. There is (2) no Quality Assurance (QA) strategy meaning (2) its process is broken. The (2) Configuration Management (CM) system and process, in its collaboration with QA, is also broken. As such, it is possible that code gets released untested through bypassing CM. There also seems to be an accountability problem: Brightmouth Solutions do not appear to be accountable for their actions (and inactions), which means there appears to be (3) no contractual or service level agreement between supplier and customer, which is bound to bring low quality service in the long term. This is listed as a technical root cause though it has a business and customer impact. Indeed, we are not aware of the scope of this problem which could also negatively affect the relationship between Brightmouth and the agency help desks. It's something to explore further.

Outlet Staff: there is a (4) lack of a software release strategy, making it (5) impossible to inform Help Desk and (6) introduce change prior to roll out via outlet staff training, having the knock on effect that customers are delayed and errors are more easily made in the customer transaction.

Help Desks: are seen to be (1) using different systems and not working together. There is (5) no single agreed communications protocol, which means there is no clear and consistent process for reporting and responding to incidents. How should a help desk report the severity of an incident to Brightmouth? This needs to be resolved.

Question 4 is the opportunity to address those root cause problems.
Technology: Four interviewees recommended (4) implementing well defined communication protocols between all the partners. That is, there needs to be a communication protocol for incident reporting, escalation and response between the Agency – via the Help Desk – and Brightmouth Solutions. There also needs to be a communication protocol for Help Desks and Outlet Staff.

There are noted problems in how software is released (2 responses). This is an opportunity (5) to introduce a tailored release management strategy in how Brightmouth Solutions releases software into the Agency. This means that Brightmouth needs (5) to implement a testing strategy, in this case, particularly around Regression testing. That strategy should also (5) fix and clarify the configuration management process to ensure there are no version control and release issues again.

One final technical concern is the level of service that Brightmouth can be held accountable for. Currently there appears to be almost no accountability. A best practice would be to (6) introduce a comprehensive service level agreement (SLA) between Brightmouth and the Agency. An SLA acts like a contract between the two parties to state expected levels of service and performance, and at what cost to the Agency. The Agency also wants to introduce punishment clauses in the event of a preventable failure. Clearly the Agency views this technical failure – printer and server meltdown – to have been preventable. But because there appears to have been no provision for an SLA or contract regarding service levels, there isn't much that the Agency can do to get compensation other than to tear up the existing contract it has with Brightmouth. Though this is an option that has been discussed, politically it isn't expedient to do this now, though we have not been told a reason why. We might not wish to consider a single response like this in an interview except that it is coming from a senior executive and the charge is pretty serious. If there is no agreed statement of service, of managing service failures and ultimately penalty clauses for failure – though this is normally beyond a sensible SLA – then there is always going to be a difference of opinion over what service quality is acceptable between the service provider and its client that will be hard to resolve.

Customers: The key opportunity to improve customer relations when these problems arise is to (4) implement a communication protocol for both Outlet Staff and Help Desk staff in providing feedback and updates to Customers. Another opportunity that will improve the Customer's lot would be (8) better change management procedures when new software and features are introduced. This would (7) give outlet staff time to learn the new system without cutting into customer contact time. It would also give Help Desk staff the opportunity to notify outlet staff well in advance of the upcoming change.

Help Desk: the issue of three different help desks has been raised. The opportunity to resolve this is simply (1) to consolidate the help desks into one. There's no need to remove the three phone numbers provided those all come into the same desk. To make matters even more straightforward, it is sensible to (2) have a single incident management system.

Please note that table 5 does not provide an exhaustive list of 'Opportunities'. Instead, it simply provides some example recommendations.

Table 5. Root Cause Analysis Results

#	Impacts	Symptoms	Root Causes	Opportunity
1	Technical: Printers and servers froze causing 30-40 minute delay in printing licenses.	Code released untested; process problems. Brightmouth lack of accountability.	(1) No QA strategy, process broken; (2) CM system process broken and bypassed regularly. (3) Unclear service level contract or agreement between Brightmouth Solutions and Agency.	(1) Introduce release management strategy; (2) Implement regression testing strategy within an agreed QA framework; (3) Fix and standardize the configuration management process; (4) Introduce formalised service level agreements between the Agency and

			Brightmouth.
2	Customer: left queuing for hours, could not renew licenses in time, meaning some lost jobs and / or arrested and fined for driving unlicensed vehicles or without a license.	Outlet staff not updated about situation or fixes so cannot inform customer; expected to self-learn new software on the job causing delays / errors.	(1) Lack of software release strategy making it (2) impossible to inform Help Desk and train staff in the change prior to roll out.	(5) Establish communications protocol for Help Desk and Outlet Staff in responding to Customers; (6) Introduce a change management structure that allows acceptable time for staff training on new system / features prior to roll out.
3	Help Desk: outlet staff not being told how to respond; escalation ignored; inconsistent response to customers.	Too many (three) help desks; poor severity identification and no single process for escalation; unclear who has to respond at Brightmouth; recording of incidents haphazard by Help Desk – Brightmouth unaware of severity of problem; help desk ineffective in	(1) Help desks using different systems, not collaborating; (2) no single agreed communications protocol to Brightmouth, outlet staff and others and (3) no clear mechanism for the reporting of severity of incidents.	(7) Consolidated single help desk (can still have different phone numbers); (8) single incident management system; (9) Establish communications protocol between Help Desk and Outlet Staff; (10) Establish communications protocol between Help Desk and Brightmouth

	informing staff in advance of new release – Desk only knows night before.			Solutions for managing incidents and responses.

As can be seen, it makes sense to not only conduct a content analysis on a post-mortem review but also to organise your responses into table 5. It also makes sense to structure the impacts in terms of area of impact. We've done that for Technical, Customer and Help Desk impact. Though technical impact is fairly loose in scope because a technical failure ultimately affects customers and staff alike and in different ways, the purpose of such a definition is to bring focus on more technical problems, such as the release management strategy and the Quality Assurance process that can be addressed by changing practices and processes within the IT department. Other root cause problems such as non-existent or poorly defined and executed communication protocols cut across all areas. This is a globally systemic failure that needs a cultural change as much as a technical one.

So that's the table. Is it possible and desirable to do any graphical modelling? Well, that's debatable. It's always possible to produce a model. If you think about it, the opportunities identified in table 5 can be viewed as the goals and strategies for a strategic initiative to implement the opportunities. Producing a straightforward, understandable and informative model adds greatly to the comprehensibility of your findings, to their value and to yours. So if you have time to produce a model I would. (You can read at length how this is done in [1]). Here's how I might model the opportunities. The first step is to place the opportunities into strategy table:

Table 6. Strategy for Opportunities

Business Strategy (Op #) refers to Opportunity in table 5	Main Partner	Supporting Partners	Helps Achieve
Goals (G#)			
G1. Agreed service levels (Op 4)	Agency	Brightmouth Solutions	-
G2. Consolidated single help desk (Op 7)	Help Desk	Customers, Outlet Staff, Brightmouth Solutions	G1
G3. Single incident management system (Op 8)	Help Desk	Customers, Outlet Staff, Brightmouth Solutions	G2
G4. Introduce a change management structure that allows acceptable time for staff training on new system / features prior to roll out (Op 6)	Help Desk	Outlet Staff	G1
Strategies (S#)			
S1. Introduce release management strategy (Op 1)	Brightmouth Solutions	Agency	G4
S2. Establish communications protocol for Help Desk and Outlet Staff in responding to Customers (Op 5)	Agency	Outlet Staff, Help Desk, Customers	G2
Tactics (T#)			
T1. Implement regression testing strategy within an agreed QA framework (Op 2)	Brightmouth Solutions	-	S1
T2. Fix and standardize the configuration management	Brightmouth Solutions	-	S1

process (Op 3)			
T3. Establish communications protocol between Help Desk and Outlet Staff (Op 9)	Agency	Outlet Staff, Help Desk	S2
T4. Establish communications protocol between Help Desk and Brightmouth Solutions for managing incidents and responses (Op 10)	Agency	Brightmouth Solutions, Help Desk	S2

The next step is to produce a goal model and this is shown in figure 3 below. The benefit of producing such a model is potentially quite substantial but this must be weighed with the time and effort it takes to produce one. The upward arrows in figure 2 indicate 'contributes to the achievement of' so that Goal 3 'Single incident management system' contributes to or helps achieve Goal 2 'Consolidated single help desk'.

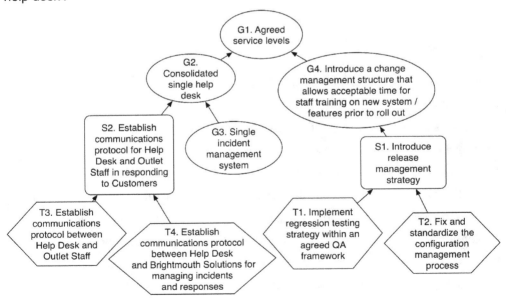

Figure 2. Strategy model of Opportunities

Figure 2 provides a different view of the opportunities and a degree of structure that is not always easy to identify from a table. The client will have the final say on whether the model is of value. You might ask whether Goal 4 is really a goal at all. It looks similar to the strategies so could be relabelled a strategy. Why is Tactic 4 contributing to Strategy 2? Could it be the other way round? Again, this is the whole point of producing the models, to do analysis, to come to a better understanding of the problem and the solution.

As before, we need to also consider responsibilities for the achievement of the goals, strategies and tactics. This is done in a partner strategy model as seen in figure 3.

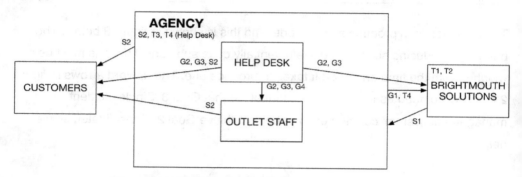

Figure 3. Strategic Partners model of Opportunities

The Strategic Partners model in figure 3 puts the strategies, goals and tactics into a context. It becomes much clear who is responsible for the delivery of a strategy and who else is involved. The model is easy to read: Brightmouth Solutions is responsible for delivering Strategy 1 and this is shown in figure 3 by placing the S1 label closest to Brightmouth. The arrowhead to a strategic partner indicates this is the recipient of and partner in achieving the strategy, goal and / or tactic, though the main responsibility falls on the originator. Brightmouth is also responsible for implementing Tactics 1 and 2 internally so this has no obvious impact on the other partners. However, failure to implement these tactics could see a failure is delivering on Strategy 1, introduce release management strategy into the Agency. This would have a potential knock on effect in that it would be unlikely to have a reliable change management practice for the Help Desk and Outlet Staff (Goal 4) – because they would never be certain of release dates or its management (Strategy 1), nor the quality of the released software (Tactics 1 and 2). Without any of these, it seems certain that agreeing service levels would not be realistic or at least the service levels would not be realistically achieved. Should we rename the partner 'Outlet Staff' to simply 'Outlets' or should we have both or stick with just staff?

You see what is happening here? All of a sudden we can begin to put a story together around those opportunities; there are also holes and doubts but that's the point of analysis, to help you find the holes and doubts and plug them. This was possible just with table 5 and with the inclusion of the models it has become much clearer and easier to do. Modelling will always add value so long as you do it in a straightforward and readable way.

Report

The following presents a final draft report you might submit to your client. I do not include the tables and models already shown above. Please refer to them if required.

Brightmouth Solutions Post-Mortem Review DRAFT Final Report
DRAFT for discussion 26-9-2016
Author: Karl Cox

Background
The purpose of this report is to:
- Identify key impacts of system failure in the Agency outlet offices.
- Identify activities, processes and actions that contributed to the failure in both the Agency and Brightmouth.
- Establish root causes for the failure: systemic poor or missing practices in both the Agency and Brightmouth.
- Propose opportunities for practice improvement that will nullify or eliminate the root causes.

Context

Brightmouth Solutions is a software provider that delivers cloud and web systems to government agencies. The latest software release at the Agency caused severe problems over one hundred customer-facing Agency offices, bringing them to a standstill. Customers were then unable to complete their business before the end of the tax year causing some of them to run into potential financial penalties, some arrests and loss of jobs. Karl Land Ltd has been hired to identify the root causes of the failure, their impact and propose viable contextual long-term solutions to eradicate the root causes.

Scope of the report

This draft final report reflects the thoughts and opinions of all pre-selected interview candidates plus three others considered significant by interviewees. The range of roles covers C-level to operational staff at the Agency and Brightmouth as well as Agency customers. This final report is a draft for discussion purposes only.

Interviewee List

Brightmouth Solutions:

- Mike, General Manager IT
- Phil, Quality Assurance Manager
- Ann, Configuration Manager
- Wendy, Project Manager
- Bob, Lead Developer

Agency:

- Pete, Senior Executive for Customer Relations
- Andie, Brightmouth Liaison
- Nikky, Help Desk Manager
- Fred, Help Desk Operative
- Stevie, Outlet Operator
- Sarah, Outlet Operator
- Mark, Outlet Manager
- ...

Customers:

- Five customer representatives were interviewed.

Structure of the Report

The report has the following structure:

Section 1 presents Key Findings in Brief for Brightmouth Solutions post-mortem review:

- Impacts
- Symptoms
- Root causes
- Opportunities.

Section 2 presents a breakdown and description of impacts, symptoms, root causes and opportunities that emerged from the interviews.

Section 3 presents more detail on the opportunities and outlines a strategic initiative to introduce those opportunities identified in Brightmouth Solutions and the Agency. The Appendix lists:

- Supporting data for the models presented in section 3.
- Supporting evidence.
- 'How To Read the Models'.

Section 1: Key Findings in Brief

- Impact:
    - Customers unable to renew licenses.
    - Customers as a consequence ran risk of acting illegally: some customers arrested and fined for driving without a license.
    - Printers and servers froze in outlet offices: 30-40 minute delay in transaction processing.
- Symptoms:
    - Uncertainty in communication protocol between help desks at Agency and Brightmouth.
    - Reporting methods vary between Help Desks.

- o Brightmouth IT failures: easy to bypass the configuration management and quality assurance processes.
  - o No outlet staff training is contributory to the failure.
  - o Little to zero feedback from staff to customers.
- Root causes:
  - o Gaps in testing process at Brightmouth.
  - o No single help desk system.
  - o Communication protocols and responses lacking between Brightmouth and Agency in emergency situation.
- Opportunities:
  - o Standardised quality assurance and configuration management practice as part of structured release management lifecycle.
  - o Single point of contact help desk.
  - o Service Level Agreement between Brightmouth and Agency to determine and put into measureable practice the roles, responsibilities and actions for communication and response between the two parties.

Section 2: Detailed Findings

Table 5 (see above) lists the major impacts felt by the failure, the symptoms that contributed to that failure and the root causes of those failures. The final column presents opportunities for introducing new practices or changing existing practices to bring about improvement and eliminate those root causes of failure.

Table 5 is organised into themes across rows. The themes are general areas of highest impact: technical failure, customer impact and help desk confusion. All symptoms, root causes and opportunities refer to the specific area of impact. Note there is a chain reaction in terms of impact and this is reflected in the table: the technical failure caused chaos in the outlet offices that put customers in trouble legally and the response from the Agency was inadequate because of its help desk failings.

What People Said

Mike, General Manager of IT at Brightmouth Solutions, User Relations Board technical advisor

Interviewed 12th August 2016 by Karl Cox and A.N. Other

Quotes:

"We got the notification from our customer [of printer and server failures] and then decided it wasn't high priority so sat on it."

"I only fathomed there was a real problem when... my sister told me about her license woes over Sunday dinner. I thought she was exaggerating when she said she'd been queuing for four hours and had then given up. But I checked it out with a couple of the outlet managers and found a big fat mess."

Key Points

- Impact: Servers and printers slowed to standstill: 30-40 minute delay for customers; customers fined, arrested, lost jobs.
- Symptom: Help desks did not provide adequate information about incidents.
- Symptom: Issues with quality assurance and configuration management processes: code released without being tested.
- Root cause: help desks not collaborating; QA and CM processes broken and easily bypassed.
- Opportunities: Single help desk; single system to improve communication between Brightmouth and the Government Agency; fix the release management cycle.

Section 3: Opportunities

Table 7 presents the opportunities identified together with a set of key considerations for implementing those opportunities. The key considerations explain some of the details around the opportunities.

Table 7. Opportunities and Key Considerations

#	Opportunity	Key Considerations
1	Introduce release management strategy (Brightmouth and Agency).	• Eradicate ingrained, silo, project management perspective for release management (within Brightmouth). • Both the Agency and Brightmouth manage release end-to-end through each appointing a release manager. • Ensure a single release management milestone schedule. • Implement release steering committee to approve changes, impact assessments and go/no go decisions (both Brightmouth and Agency).
2	Implement regression testing strategy within an agreed QA framework (Brightmouth).	• Introduce industry standard regression testing, including necessary tools. • Ensure regression testing covers all key interfaces and related systems within Quality Assurance. • Define strategy for managing user acceptance tests and acceptance criteria. • Virtualization strategy: create environments much faster and reduce number of required servers.
3	Fix and standardize the configuration management process (Brightmouth).	• Define where each project is in the software development lifecycle and acceptable risk of missing release date. • Reassess Configuration Management process to handle promotion and maintenance of environments.
4	Introduce service level agreements between the Agency and	• Brightmouth and Agency agreement on accountabilities and resources for warranty periods post-release. • Agree on processes and service levels for support,

	Brightmouth.	impact assessment, determining what gets fixed and what gets packaged for maintenance.
		• Implement lifecycle of agreement, monitoring and reporting.
		• Also, establish Operational Level Agreements between different parts of Brightmouth Solutions so that:
		  - Roles and responsibilities are clearly defined (Customer Liaison and IT).
		  - Procedures for work between different IT units are followed (Configuration Management, Quality Assurance and Development).

5	Establish communications protocol for Help Desk and Outlet Staff in responding to Customers.	• Clear communications protocols between Help Desk and Outlet Staff:
		  - Response times.
		  - Escalation process.
		  - Feedback including workarounds.
		  - Response criteria from Outlet Staff to Customers.

6	Introduce a change management structure that allows acceptable time for staff training on new system / features prior to roll out.	• Business change decision makers accountable for operational success.
		• Ensure change is clear and consistent Outlet Office implementation process:
		  - Standard staff training processes.
		  - Impact assessment.
		  - Business interpretation – staff can interpret change in a business manner rather than a technical one.
		• Single repository of release information accessible by Outlet Offices.
		• Standard notice period and lead time.

7	Consolidated single Help Desk (can still have different phone numbers provided they all go to the same Help Desk).	• Clear communication protocols between Outlet Offices and Help Desk:
		  - Use of wiki/intranet/bulletin boards to notify Outlet Staff of communication procedures.
		  - Clear escalation process with explicit feedback loop.
		• Designated problem manager at Help Desk responsible for identifying and managing problem resolution.

8	Single incident management system.	• Use of a single system for issues and ticket referencing. • All incoming and outgoing calls to be logged. • Single reporting channel for issues and fixes to Outlet Staff based upon ticketing system.

9	Establish communications protocol between Help Desk and Outlet Staff.	• Clear communications protocols between Help Desk and Outlet Staff for day-to-day work activities:
		  - Response times.
		  - Escalation process.
		  - Feedback including workarounds.

10	Establish communications protocol between Help Desk and Brightmouth Solutions for managing incidents and responses.	• Clear communications protocols between Help Desk and Brightmouth:
		  - Preset response times.
		  - Escalation process via clear identification of incident-to-problem.
		  - Feedback loop explaining workarounds.

[Comment: The content of table 7 is important for you: the case for change must be made. You will need to elaborate upon the opportunities. Also, you'll need to present the outline of a plan for change. The plan does not have to be detailed. If fact, it pays to be a bit loose because you want your client to 'think of' the plan; your job is to put the seed of the idea into his head. This is where you earn your stripes as a consultant. You might be asked to propose a change in direction in more detail and this is the opportunity to use strategic models [1] as a means of expressing the opportunities.]

Brightmouth Solutions Strategic Initiative
Figures 2 and 3 (above) presents a goal hierarchy and context for implementing necessary opportunities into Brightmouth and the Agency.

Appendices
The following appendices present supporting materials and data.
Appendix A: Brightmouth Solutions Business Strategy Table (see Table 6 above).
[End of Report]

Concluding Remarks

It may not be necessary to include goal and context models so that is up to you. However, I do think in this case the idea of hierarchy is of some benefit so the goal model makes sense. Also the context and where goal responsibility sits is also good. I included the outline of a draft report in case you are in the position where you need to write a formal document about your post-mortem review. Use the one here as a template if you like.

The idea of a post-mortem review is not to find out who made mistakes and fire them, or to apportion blame, or as a step in taking legal action. It is solely to uncover where practices and processes can be improved so that the same mistake does not happen twice. It needs to be inclusive so that those staff who are part of the review process should not feel they are about to be burnt at the stake. Include them in figuring out solutions and ask them where they know some small steps can make a big difference next time round.

About the author

Karl A. Cox, PhD, is a Senior Lecturer at the University of Brighton, in the School of Computing, Engineering and Mathematics. He has taught business-IT alignment and IT project management to undergraduates and postgraduates for close to 20 years and has published over 80 articles and book chapters on the subject of IT and business requirements, alignment, processes and project management. Karl has also consulted to companies in the UK, Australia and Japan. He owned a consulting business in Australia specialising in business-IT alignment, and was a senior research scientist at NICTA, Ltd, in Australia. Whilst there, his focus was on the commercial development of methods to improve business-IT alignment, as well as conduct consulting and research engagements with companies across Australia and in Japan.

Bibliography

[1] Karl A. Cox (2015), Strategic Requirements Analysis: from interviews to models, Routledge, ISBN: 978-1472474728

www.ingramcontent.com/pod-product-compliance
Lightning Source LLC
Chambersburg PA
CBHW060928050326
40689CB00013B/3011

* 9 7 8 1 5 3 7 7 9 5 6 0 7 *